FINDING PEACE
After the Loss of a Loved Animal Companion

Written by
Diane Pomerance, Ph.D.
Illustrated by Trey Wright

POLAIRE PUBLICATIONS
Flower Mound, Texas

Copyright 2006 by Diane Pomerance, Ph.D.

All rights reserved. No part of this book may be reproduced by any information storage and retrieval system or transmitted in any form or by any means, electronic, mechanical, photocopying, recording or otherwise, except by a reviewer who may quote brief passages or reproduce illustrations in a review, without written permission of the publisher.

Printed in the United States of America
First Printing: 2006

10 09 08 07 010 1 2 3 4 5

Cover and text illustrations by Trey Wright
Book design by Diane Pomerance, Ph.D.
and Crystal Wood, Tattersall Publishing, Denton, Texas
Author Photo by Don Barnes/The Photographers

For information, write to:
Polaire Publications
PMB 217
2221 Old Justin Rd., Ste. 119
Flower Mound, Texas 75028

www.animalcompanionsandtheirpeople.com

ISBN-13: 978-0-9708500-5-8
ISBN-10: 0-9708500-5-0

Library of Congress Control Number: 2006902140

Dedication

This book is dedicated to Sophie—the most loving, humble, generous and beautiful canine spirit I have ever known. A dachshund-beagle mix, Sophie's ability to love and express her love for every other creature, including human beings, was unparalleled. She was the dearest of friends and companions: loyal, devoted, steadfast and courageous. She was a great guide and an astute teacher. To know her was one of the greatest blessings of my life.

My husband and I found Sophie on a five-lane highway near Houston, Texas. She was darting in and out of traffic, and we were terrified that she would be hit by a car. But, somehow, in an answer to our fervent prayers, perhaps, she managed to cross the road safely. It was July and terribly hot and humid, and Sophie was painfully thin and dehydrated. She was filthy and smelly, apparently having been on the road for a while, but her tail wagged and wagged. She was very friendly and she readily allowed us to pick her up and put her in our car. Within a few moments, this small, black-and-tan dog had become a beloved member of our family.

(continued)

Sophie became my first Canine Good Citizen and Animal Assisted Therapy Dog. She loved and shared her love with everyone she met. She visited the infirm and elderly at hospitals and assisted living centers. She played and forged a unique bond with special-needs children and adults. She shared her extraordinary ability to heal, comfort, and console those who were grieving.

For so many years, Sophie seemed tireless, but as she grew older, she was diagnosed with Cushing's Disease, a severe heart murmur, numerous secondary infections, several small strokes, and other health problems that finally took their toll upon this gentle, unceasingly loving soul. Her tail never stopped wagging from the time we first met her until several days before she died on November 12, 2005.

It is to my Sophie, who brought me so much joy and comfort, that I dedicate this book, *Finding Peace*. My husband always referred to Sophie as our "guru" dog, for she taught us so much about Life and helped guide us on our own journey to find Peace. She was always content, at peace, and knew better than any being I've ever known the true meaning of Unconditional Love.

Acknowledgments

It is a privilege to recognize and acknowledge the remarkable group of new as well as old friends and colleagues of mine who sacrifice so much to save and improve the quality of the lives of our animal companions. These courageous, generous and compassionate people work tirelessly and unceasingly to rescue and help abandoned, neglected, and abused animals. They do their best to alleviate suffering and to help animals in need recover from often deplorable, unthinkably horrific, and heartbreaking circumstances. They provide medical attention as well as loving kindness. They then help to find these animals safe, secure, and happy homes in which they will receive the love, respect, and care that they so deserve and need.

Our animal companions love us unconditionally. The people in Rescue and Animal Welfare work come remarkably close to reciprocating this love.

We have always been a part of the natural world. The wonder and beauty, intricacy and efficiency, power and peace of Nature are within us and are inextricably woven into the fabric of our being. The grandeur and majesty, the fragility and vulnerability, the sublime and inexplicable essence of Nature are to be found within all human beings and all living creatures. The world of Nature is an integral and vital link to who we are and the realm of the Divine. From the world of Nature, we have received and continue to receive an understanding of the extraordinary beauty and complexity of Life. Through Nature, our spirits are elevated. Yet, sadly, many of us have lost awareness of this relationship—this connectedness—and contact with the creative, healing, restorative and regenerative power of the world of Nature.

Where there once was harmony, there now is discord; where there was resonance, there is dissonance; where there once existed a balance between Nature and man, there is at present a great imbalance wherein humans, by means of sheer numbers and technology, seemingly exercise the vast majority of power and control over all aspects of life on Earth. While we have accomplished much in the way of technology and invention, we have lost touch with our true nature and purpose for existing on Earth. Where we once revered Mother Nature, we have reviled her and tried to alter, manipulate, and even dominate her, wreaking havoc on the planet and in so many of our lives. Ceasing to respect and honor her, we have arrogantly assumed superiority over her and carelessly disregarded her laws and power. Somehow we have forgotten that it is through Nature that we are reborn, revived, renewed—it is through Nature that we receive healing, hope, and vitality.

Somehow, we seem to have lost our way and our identities as Spiritual Beings above all else. We have become a society bowed by our awe and worship of technology and man's cleverness and resourcefulness—man's inventions and achievements. So many of us are unaware of our connection to and relationship with Nature and our Creator. We are instead focused upon the external, scintillating, superficial, material, scientific and mathematical. We live apart from one another—lonely and isolated—unable to communicate genuinely and share heartfelt and meaningful relationships, or to grasp any real understanding of love.

There are so many of us who are alone and lonely, who are separated from loved ones, friends and family members. No longer members of strong nuclear families and religious institutions or stable, supportive neighborhoods and communities, we find ourselves more mobile than ever before. We move or relocate to other communities, cities, countries or continents. We may find ourselves isolated, detached, and alienated from those around us. We watch television, listen to the radio or go to the movies. Often, if not solely, many of us turn to our computers or the Internet or other technology for our "relationships." Others of us are more fortunate, and even if we don't find inspiring relationships among other people, we find real love, affection, friendship, companionship, camaraderie, and loyalty through the animal companions we adopt—those with whom we forge a bond and with whom we share our hearts, our lives, and our homes.

Our animal companions serve as a link to Nature and the natural world. They provide us with so many gifts, and are even beneficial to our health—physiologically, psychologically, emotionally, and spiritually. They can improve the quality and increase the longevity of our lives. From them we may learn love and affection, beauty and grace, dignity and stoicism, patience and perseverance. They seem to be able to empathize with us, sharing joy and sorrow, success and failure, triumph and defeat. They may even help us make new friends and can serve as a means of linking us to and with other people and creatures.

Our animal companions love and accept us just as we are. They do not lie, embellish, fabricate, or pretend to be what they are not. They do not judge, blame, criticize, or condemn us. They readily forgive our idiosyncrasies, foibles, and flaws. They love us unconditionally. They bring us laughter and joy, gaiety and spontaneity, frivolity and entertainment, in addition to providing us with a sense of comfort and well-being. They enrich our lives in so many ways—providing support, encouragement, forgiveness, healing, empathy, and grace. And they are sentient beings with whom we communicate in a language that transcends mere words.

For so many of us, our animal companions are family members who share our everyday lives and routines with us—wake-up time, meals, work and playtime, exercise and bedtime; they eat and sleep with us. They socialize and interact with us and our friends and family members. They spend weekends, holidays, and special occasions with us. They accompany us on walks and on our errands. They travel with us, and we even bring them with us on our vacations. They curl up by our sides or at our feet when we're on the telephone or at the computer, when we're reading, listening to music, or watching television. By virtue of their mere presence in our homes, they are a cozy, comfortable and comforting presence who are exposed to, and, to some degree, are familiar with the wide range of emotions and activities we experience.

As do we, our animal companions eventually grow old. Perhaps we initially adopted them as a puppy or kitten, as an infant or young animal. We observe and enjoy their youthful playfulness, exuberance, inquisitiveness, and almost reckless abandon. They seem invincible and inexhaustible. However, as our animal friends mature and age at a far more rapid rate than do we, as they get older we notice both the subtle and obvious changes in their personalities, appearance and behaviors. Inevitably, the older they become, the more physical and physiological limitations and challenges they face. Regular exercise, prudent and healthy diet, plenty of interaction with us and other loving humans and animal siblings and friends, along with frequent visits to the veterinarian can ease discomfort or pain and help improve the quality as well as increase the longevity of a pet's life. And yet, as in the case with human beings, physical illnesses, disabilities, and infirmities arise as the pet ages. She will require additional compassion, patience, and care on the part of her owners. The pet may require special medical care and medication, surgery, radiation or chemotherapy, frequent visits to the vet, vitamins, dietary supplements, special diets, physical therapy, and so on.

Eventually the dreaded day will arrive when in our hearts we know that our beloved animal companion is old, weak, frail and fragile, and will not be with us much longer. When our pets are diagnosed with a serious or critical injury or illness, or have a terminal or untreatable disease; when they are obviously suffering or in pain that cannot be diminished or alleviated; when they withdraw from our presence and prefer to isolate themselves and be alone; when they are no longer interested in eating the special treats they once eagerly anticipated and immediately devoured; when they no longer show an interest in playing the games and with the toys that used to entrance and delight them; when they become immobile and incontinent; when it is obvious that they are no longer experiencing a life of quality; we realize that it is time to let them go, mercifully and unselfishly. It is time to release them from the shackles of their worn-out physical bodies and to provide them a merciful, humane, gentle, and compassionate end to their suffering. We may make the decision to have our animal euthanized, to provide them with the "good death" that the term implies.

After considerable thought, prayer, and deliberation, after studying and researching the subject and procedure of euthanasia, we may make one of the most complex and difficult, yet kindest and most compassionate, decisions we may ever have to make. With the aid of a trusted and experienced veterinarian, we have the life of our aging, suffering, or terminally ill animal companion mercifully, quickly, and humanely brought to an end.

We may have agonized about our animal's health problems and impending death, as well as the decision to euthanize him, for a long while. As our animal's condition has worsened, we experience so many overwhelming emotions, ranging from sadness and despair to anger, bitterness, frustration, anxiety and deep depression. We have tried so very hard to be of help to our pet; to provide love, comfort, care and support; to make certain he is getting proper veterinary care; that he is being fed properly and appropriately, that he is receiving his medication, and so on. We have served on-call night and day to minister to his needs; we have made many late-night or early-morning visits to the veterinary emergency room, and frequent visits to our regular vet; and yet, despite all our efforts, we are unable to help our friend. We have known that his death is imminent, and yet we dread and fear the day when he will no longer be with us physically. No matter how much we comprehend intellectually, we are overcome by emotion and engulfed by fear, heartache, and a profound sadness.

After our beloved animal companion has died and is physically "gone"—whether he has died of natural causes or has been euthanized, and after we have made the decision to cremate or bury his remains—we are faced with a new and formidable emotional challenge: the experience of *grief* over our loss…a searing, powerful, and overwhelming confluence of sadness, anguish, despair, pain, desperation, emptiness, and loneliness. We are overcome by many emotions. There is now a deep, undeniable void in our hearts and lives. The beloved one who for so long has been loyally, patiently, lovingly, and steadfastly by our side is no longer there. Our hearts ache—yearn—for his

presence, for just one more opportunity to hold and hug him, to scratch behind his ears, to toss him the ball with which he played and slept, to rest our head on his. The sadness is intense and immeasurable. Even if we live with other people and animals, the silence created by the absence of our deceased friend in our home is almost unendurable. We feel as though we are all alone; our one true friend—the one who knew us best—is gone. No one else seems to feel just as we do. No one else seems to understand the depth or intensity of our relationship with our animal companion. No one, not even our closest friends or family members, seems to have the words that will console, comfort, and lift our heavy heart and spirit. We hear it said over and over like a taunting refrain, "It was only a dog, a cat, an animal. You can get another one." But our relationship with our pet was unique. There was a remarkable bond that existed between us. We wonder how we will ever recover from this profound loss. We wonder *why* our pet has been taken from us. *Why* are we in such pain? *Why* do all living creatures die? *Why* has God forsaken us?

When a beloved animal companion dies, we are faced with an overwhelming sense of loss, and our faith and belief in God and our religion may be tested. We have so many questions: questions about the meaning of life and its purposefulness; questions about death and what death signifies. Is death permanent? Do animals have souls that survive physical death? Do our pets go to heaven? Will we ever be reunited with them? Why do we live and die? Why has God taken such an innocent creature from us? It is common to experience bitterness, guilt and anger with God and ourselves. We feel so helpless and alone. We seem to have so little control over our destiny and the lives of our pets. What purpose has our pet's life served? Our lives and emotions are awhirl—everything has been turned topsy-turvy. We may cry uncontrollably and continually; we may feel physically ill; we may feel restless and find ourselves unable to focus or concentrate on the tasks at hand. We may sleep too

little or too much; we may lose our appetites or eat to excess. We may be absent-minded and forgetful; we may believe that we hear or see the deceased. We may feel relief that the sick or dying pet has found peace. We have so many conflicting emotions. We may erupt in anger over minor irritations; we may wish to be left alone and have no contact with others. We find ourselves deeply sad, disillusioned, despondent and discouraged. Our lives may seem purposeless, empty, meaningless, and futile. We feel as though we have lost everything that matters to us. We no longer care about our jobs or even other relationships. We may not wish to continue to live. We feel hopeless, anxious, and depressed. All of these feelings are manifestations of our grief—the grief caused by the loss of our beloved pet.

For many of us, the loss of a loved one comes as a great shock or surprise, even though we have intellectually understood that our friend was dying; for others of us, loss is a far-too-familiar painful and tragic occurrence in our lives. Yet, for many of us, the loss of our one true and constant friend—one who is pure of heart, faithful, and full of love—can somehow be the most devastating and disturbing of all. For this friend knows us better than any other. This one has shared our deepest feelings, most cherished dreams and most intimate secrets. This one has readily forgiven us for all our "mistakes" and transgressions, and has accepted us joyously and unconditionally *just as we are.*

When our beloved animal companion dies, we are left with a gaping hole in our hearts and lives. The pain can be numbing and immobilizing. We realize that our hearts have been broken by the loss of this simple, humble, loving presence. Our beloved companion is gone. It is the end of one era of our lives; it is also the beginning of a new one.

Many of us have been ill prepared and inadequately socialized to understand the grieving process, and we are extremely uncomfortable and awkward at discussing the subjects of loss and death. We have been taught not to cry, as it may be construed as a sign of weakness. We have not been encouraged to share openly and honestly or discuss our painful, sad, or "negative" experiences and emotions, as they are generally regarded as distasteful and can cause listeners embarrassment or discomfort. The advice we have received is to hide or subvert our feelings and to "keep a stiff upper lip," to "pull ourselves up by our bootstraps," and to "carry on." Our friends and family members and co-workers are uncomfortable discussing grief; they have not been educated as to what are helpful and comforting words and actions. They tell us "We know how you feel" (when it is blatantly obvious they do not); they advise us to "get another dog or cat" and to "move on with our lives." Those who are grieving or mourning derive little, if any, comfort from such well-intentioned platitudes as: "All things must pass"; "Time will heal"; "Be grateful you have another dog or cat"; "He's in a better place"; "She led a full life"; "The living must go on"; "Be grateful you had her for so long"; "Keep busy"; "Grieve alone." The loss of a pet can be especially difficult because there are so many people in our society that do not understand or acknowledge how powerful and significant a bond can exist between a person and his or her animal companion. Nor are there the commonly accepted and public comforting rituals such as funerals, memorial services, and wakes held on behalf of animals.

Unfortunately, most of us have not been taught that grief is one of life's most painful, intense, complex, and misunderstood emotional experiences, and that, at the same time, it is the

natural, normal, and healthy response to loss. There are many, many losses that precipitate or result in grief—for example, the death of a spouse, sibling, child, or pet; divorce or separation; moving from one place to another; graduation; marriage; loss of profession or social position; retirement; "empty nest"; health problems; financial or legal problems; loss of trust or safety; loss of faith in God, etc. All of us experience many losses throughout our lives. Although we are reluctant to acknowledge it, loss is an inevitable part of life on earth. And grief is cumulative—in other words, the intensity of grief we may experience over the loss of a beloved pet may depend on the strength and intensity of the bond that existed between our pet and ourselves, as well as how many other losses we have previously sustained and from which we have recovered in our lives thus far.

It is healthy for us to acknowledge openly and honestly and to express all of our feelings—and that we are missing and grieving the loss of one we dearly and truly loved—one who has greatly enriched and enhanced our lives; one whose love will never be forgotten; one whose spirit, friendship, and camaraderie will remain in our hearts, souls, and lives forever. We should not be ashamed or embarrassed to express our true feelings to friends and family members or to others who are sympathetic and empathetic. It is healthy for us to discuss our loss with other people who are compassionate, supportive, sympathetic, and empathetic. We can review, reflect upon, and celebrate the gifts our animal companions have given us and the lessons they have taught us.

We are able to derive comfort and solace, as well as heightened spiritual awareness and grace, through our contact with Nature and the natural world. Through the wonder and beauty of Nature, we come into contact with the Divine Power and Creator/Creative Force of All Life. We can partake of the healing, strengthening, and revitalizing power of the physical as well as the spiritual sunlight, and become increasingly aware of the beauty and inevitability of the cycles and Circle of Life. It is a testament to our faith and spirituality as to how we regard and respond to these cycles—to birth and death in particular.

As we come to realize that our beloved animal companion is dead and that she is not coming back again, we begin to grieve her loss. The mourning process begins. It is a different process for each of us. There is no allotted duration for or method of grieving—each of us grieves differently and for varying amounts of time. Some common responses to our loss are shock, disbelief, denial, bargaining, anger, guilt, depression, and isolation. Our grief is commensurate with the quality, intensity, and quantity of time we have spent and the experiences we have shared with our beloved friend. For many of us, the initial impact of the loss of our friend can be likened to a raw, painful, and gaping wound. Then, after a while, the wound is scabbed over and bothersome but not so painful; later it is represented by a noticeable and somewhat irritating scar and some minor pain, and eventually, by a scar that is hardly discernible.

Certain actions may provide comfort and healing and recovery from grief. To identify that we are grieving is the first step in the grieving process. Recognizing that it is normal and healthy to grieve is the next step. Next, it is important to express our feelings, whether by talking to others or writing about our feelings. We may wish to keep a journal or write a letter to God, or a poem or short story in honor of our deceased pet; if we are musical we may wish to compose a song or sing in our pet's honor; if we dance or are artistic, we may compose a dance or paint our departed friend. We may begin to address our grief by honoring, memorializing, and eulogizing our pet and by holding a memorial or funeral service wherein we are able to share our feelings of sadness at our loss and to celebrate with gratitude the life that was linked to our own. We may wish to share our

memories with supportive and empathetic animal-loving friends or within the context of a grief support group.
We may wish to seek guidance from a psychologist, psychiatrist, member of the clergy, or a spiritual counselor. After the death of our pet, we must learn to be patient with and to take care of ourselves; for example, eating healthily and exercising.
We must not expect too much from ourselves. We may wish to seek answers to our questions and to read and research what various religions and philosophies teach about life and death and the immortality of both animal and human souls.

We may choose to commemorate and honor our friend's life by making a donation in her name to an animal welfare organization, or by endowing a tree or park bench or memorial plaque in her honor. We may wish to honor her memory by helping animals in need by volunteering at an animal welfare organization. We may—one day, if and when our hearts and minds tell us it's time—wish to adopt another animal in need … not to *replace,* but to *honor* the one we have loved and lost.

There is great fulfillment and satisfaction in adopting an animal that has been abandoned, neglected, or abused. The joy of contributing to their recovery and rehabilitation is indescribable. Their gratitude for living in a home where they are loved, valued, appreciated, and respected is limitless. In particular, older animals—far too often discarded or disposed of simply because of their age—offer priceless gifts and lessons to those who adopt them.

Although no other animal can or ever will replace the beloved companion we have lost, there are other beautiful, intelligent, and loving animals in desperate need of kindness, compassion, and a permanent home. These animals are vulnerable and dependent upon our generosity and our willingness to open our hearts once again to embrace and welcome them into our hearts and homes. These animals will bring special and unique gifts of their own—different from those we have received from our previous animal companions—but of indescribable and incalculable importance and meaning, nonetheless.

As we grow older and more mature, we are able to learn so many lessons about Life from our aging animal companions and to accommodate their physical, emotional, and mental infirmities, disabilities, and limitations. Yet, by observing and caring for our aging animal companion, we can learn to *accept* life's vicissitudes with grace, stoicism, and equanimity, recognizing them as inevitable and irrevocable aspects of life. We become familiar with the changes that we will invariably experience. We watch as our aging animal companions become less robust and resilient, less agile and mobile, less alert and animated; as their hearing and sight grow dimmer, as they cope with the ravages of time and receive medical treatment for diseases and illnesses that are remarkably similar to those we, as aging humans, experience.

Life continues. We learn to cope with loss: we know it is inevitable and inescapable, and that it will occur many, many times in different ways throughout our lives. It is important to understand that we are not unique in experiencing pain and suffering. We can develop tools and attitudes and a cognizance of the spiritual growth and rewards to be derived by surviving, even triumphing over, tragedy; by surviving loss and embracing Life. Out of despair comes awareness. Out of darkness, we may find our way into the Light.

During our darkest and most difficult moments, we can become quiet and still and reflect upon the Greatness of our own Being and the Divine Spark within us and all Life, the Divine Source of Light and Life. We can simply Be Still. We can close the portals of our "outer" minds to our everyday tasks and responsibilities, cares, and strife. We can seek the Deep Quietude within us. Breathing slowly and softly and absorbing into our being both the spiritual and physical Light of the Sun, which is regarded by many as the sign and symbol of God, we can focus our mind on the Creative Force, the Divine and Infinite One, and feel the Union of Spirit between Light and Life and All Living Beings. What is physical is ephemeral, fleeting. What is spiritual is lasting, timeless, and enduring.

It may be of help to contemplate the concept of life on Earth as a school of spiritual learning, training and development. We may view each of our experiences and each of our losses as a stepping-stone on the path leading us toward our mastery over the physical, emotional, mental, and spiritual aspects of Life and leading us to an ever greater awareness and understanding of the True Nature of Life and our True and Higher Selves.

In order to evolve spiritually, we face a wide range of life experiences that may be regarded as and serve as physical, mental, emotional, and spiritual "initiations." Through each of these challenges or "tests" we are given the opportunity to grow spiritually. Ultimately we seek Truth and Peace—within and without—a true and everlasting Peace.

Living on the Earth we are required to reconcile ourselves to receiving great gifts as well as coping with devastating losses. We experience joy and sorrow; the simultaneous exuberance, innocence, naiveté, self-consciousness, awkwardness, fragility, presumptuousness, and certain invincibility of youth and adolescence. As adults, we experience ambition, goal-setting, and the attempt to actualize our personal and professional aspirations. In middle age we may experience the realization of, reconciliation to, and acceptance of what *is*, our reality—what we have succeeded in mastering and what we have failed to achieve thus far—our so-called "successes" and "failures." In old age we view life differently—our dreams and goals have been altered by life experience. They may or may not have come to fruition as we envisioned them in our younger years. We may come to know ourselves far better and more about life than we did in our youth. We may experience both the grief associated with many losses and the joy of having shared many meaningful relationships throughout our lives.

With the passage of time and as we grow older, we are afforded opportunities to evolve spiritually and to expand our realm of knowledge and wisdom. We muse, ponder, explore, examine, and come to terms with the finite number of moments, hours and days that measure our allotted time on Earth. We recognize that we do not travel alone. Our journey is not solitary. It is one that is shared, enmeshed and intertwined with that of all living creatures.

We have learned that loss is inevitable and grief is cumulative, and that all of us experience countless losses throughout our lives. We lose beloved friends and family members; the familiar, beloved, and comforting presence of those with whom we have created and shared beautiful and glorious memories. Our animal companions have served as our loving, loyal, and faithful friends, teachers, and guides. Although here on Earth for only a short while, they teach us so much about Life and Death. They help us understand that no one is immune to loss. They are guides and loving companions who accompany us on the journey toward *finding Peace*. Perhaps if we did not experience pain and loss, we would not question Life's meaningfulness and purposefulness—the reasons for and significance of the events that occur in our lives and on Earth. It is during our darkest and most difficult hours that we seek aid, relief, and an end to our suffering. For many of us, it is during our darkest hours that we seek Wisdom, Understanding, and Truth.

We are creatures born of the Creative Force and in the natural world, and, as such, we die and return to our Creator and the natural world. We experience physical mortality and spiritual immortality. Our inner lives are characterized by beauty and grace and the opportunity to evolve into ever greater, more loving, tolerant, and compassionate Wiser Souls. We have the opportunity to expand our spiritual awareness and understanding. Through hard work, we can inevitably achieve spiritual mastery and the realization that true and everlasting Peace resides within our hearts. This Peace is both accessible and attainable. We *are* and always will *be*. We are ever the Creative Spirit expressing and manifesting Its *power, beauty, glory, love, wisdom* … and *Peace*.

Words of Comfort

There is no death! Our stars go down
To rise upon some fairer shore;
And bright in heaven's jeweled crown
They shine for evermore.

There is no death! The dust we tread
Shall change beneath the summer showers
To golden grain or mellow fruit,
Or rainbow-tinted flowers.

The granite rocks in powder fall,
And feed the hungry moss they bear.
The fairest leaves drink daily life
From out the viewless air.

There is no death! The leaves may fall,
The flowers may fade and pass away;
They only wait through wintry hours
The coming of the May.

And, ever near us, though unseen,
The fair immortal spirits tread;
For all the boundless universe
Is life; there are no dead!

— Edward Bulwer-Lytton

The subtlest beauties in our life
are unseen and unheard.

Kahlil Gibran

It is not the language of the painters, but the
language of Nature, to which one has to listen.

Vincent Van Gogh

Remember that you are this universe and this
universe is you.

Joy Harjo

…from the stars
and the sun
and the moon
should man learn..

Eagle Chief Letakots Lesa

I only went out for a walk and finally concluded
to stay out until sundown,
for going out, I found, was really going in.
						John Muir

When one's intelligence, mind, faith and refuge are all fixed in the Supreme, then one becomes fully cleansed of misgivings through complete knowledge and thus proceeds straight on the path of liberation.
						Bhagavad-Gita

Be still and know that I am God.
						Psalm 46:10

There is no God but God.
						The Quran

Truth is within ourselves; it takes no rise from
Outward things, what e'er you may believe.
There is an inmost center in us all,
Where truth abides in fullness; and around,
Wall upon wall, the gross flesh hems it in,
This perfect clear perception—which is truth.
A baffling and perverting carnal mesh
Binds it, and makes all error; and to know
Rather consist in opening out a way
Whence the imprisoned splendour may escape,
Than in effecting entry for a light
Supposed to be without.

Robert Browning

Smaller than the smallest,
Greater than the greatest,
This Self forever dwells
In the hearts of all.
A person freed from desire,
With mind and senses purified,
Beholds the glory of the Self
And is without sorrow.

Katha Upanishad

Everything that lives, lives not alone nor for itself.
William Blake

We bereaved are not alone. We belong to the largest company in all the world—the company of those who have known suffering.
Helen Keller

The Lord is my light and my salvation; whom shall I fear? The Lord is the strength of my life; of whom shall I be afraid?
Psalm 27:1

There is a calmness to a life lived in gratitude, a quiet joy.
Robert H. Blum

He who knows others is wise.
He who knows himself is enlightened.
Tao Te Ching

When despair for the world grows in me
and I wake in the night at the least sound
in fear of what my life and my children's
   lives may be,
I go and lie down where the wood drake
rests in his beauty on the water,
   and the great heron feeds.
I come into the peace of wild things
who do not tax their lives with forethought
of grief. I come into the presence of still water.
And I feel above me the day-blind stars
waiting with their light. For a time
   I rest in the grace of the world, and am free.

Wendell Berry

People are like stained-glass windows. They sparkle and shine when the sun is out, but when the darkness sets in, their true beauty is revealed only if there is a light from within.

Elisabeth Kubler-Ross

When a man finds no peace within himself it is useless to seek it elsewhere.

La Rouchefoliocauld

O my blessed beloved, awake!
Why do you sleep in ignorance?

                        Kabir

We know the truth not only by the reason, but by the heart.

                        Blaise Pascal

One's own thought is one's world.
What a person thinks
Is what he becomes—
That is the eternal mystery.
If the mind dwells
Within the supreme Self,
One enjoys undying happiness

                        Maitri Upanishad

God is love; and he that dwelleth in love dwelleth in God, and God in him.

                        I John 4:16

The mind is never right but when it is at
peace with itself.
Seneca

Why do you look for Him
only in churches or mosques?
Do you not see His creation?
Where does He not abide?
The whole universe made by Him
Recites His tale.
Sarmad

Nothing is ever really lost, or can be lost,
No birth, identity, form—no object of
   the world,
Nor life, nor force, nor any visible thing;
Appearance must not foil, nor shifted
   sphere confuse thy brain.
Ample are time and space—ample the
   fields of Nature.
Walt Whitman

Surely there is something in the unruffled calm of Nature that overawes our little anxieties and doubts: the sight of the deep-blue sky, and the clustering stars above, seem to impart a quiet to the mind.

Jonathan Edwards

Even such a happy Child of Earth am I:
Even as these blissful creatures do I fare;
Far from the world I walk, and from all care…

William Wordsworth

Here man is no longer the center of the world, only a witness, but a witness who is also a partner in the silent life of nature, bound by secret affinities to the trees.

Dag Hammarskjold

Thou hast made us for Thyself, and are hearts are restless until they repose in Thee.

Augustine

Just by repeating the Name,
that which cannot be understood
will be understood.
Just by repeating the Name,
that which cannot be seen
will be seen.
>*Jnaneshwar*

The first in time and the first in importance
of the influences upon the mind is that of
Nature. Every day, the sun; and, after sunset,
Night and her stars. Ever the winds blow;
ever the grass grows. Every day, men and
women, conversing, beholding and
beholden.
>*Ralph Waldo Emerson*

The earth and myself are of one mind.
The measure of the land and the measure of
our bodies are the same.
>*Joseph (Hinmaton Yalatkit),*
>*Nez Perce chief*

Do not hate or hurt anyone.
Make friends with everyone.
For your own self exists in every face.
Enjoy the sport of love.
The earth, the sky, the universe
Are all the form of the Lord,
The abode of joy.
God permeates every particle of your being.
Kabir

In the silence there is power. When anxious, when the forces of the earth threaten to overrun the soul, in the silence will come endurance. In the silence will come the breaking of the light. Be silent and know God's power and God's love…and deep soul peace.
White Eagle

Peace be to you.
Genesis 43:23

ABOUT THE AUTHOR

DIANE POMERANCE received her Ph.D. in Communications from the University of Michigan, Ann Arbor. She has been certified as a Grief Recovery Specialist by the internationally recognized Grief Recovery Institute. She was trained directly by the founder of the Institute, John W. James. Dr. Pomerance counsels those grieving from any loss; however, she has a special interest in those mourning the loss of a beloved companion animal. The loss of a pet can be devastating to adults as well as children.

Dr. Pomerance created, established, and serves as director of the Pet Grief Counseling Program for the SPCA of Texas. In addition to serving as an active volunteer for the SPCA of Texas, she is also an active member of K-9 Friends Visiting Therapy Dogs, and the Alaskan Malamute Assistance League. She is frequently interviewed as a highly qualified pet "expert" on national television and radio programs and has been interviewed in many newspapers and magazines, including the *Los Angeles Daily News*, *The Dallas Morning News*, *The Fort Worth Star-Telegram*, *Washington Times*, *Redbook*, *Quick and Simple*, and *Woman's World*. She has been an online expert for *Cat Fancy Magazine* and a guest expert on *The Montel Williams Show* and the nationally syndicated *Your Health*. She is the author of numerous articles and the highly acclaimed children's books, *When Your Pet Dies*, *Animal Companions: Your Friends, Teachers & Guides*, *Animal Companions In Our Hearts, Our Lives, and Our World* and *Animal Elders: Caring About Our Aging Animal Companions*. She lives in North Texas with her husband and many canine "kids."

ABOUT THE ILLUSTRATOR

TREY WRIGHT was born July 21, 1986, in Denton, Texas. He has enjoyed art since he was a small child, especially drawing and painting. In high school his artistic talent progressed with the help of his art teacher, Ms. Kregel, who continues to inspire him to reach his potential. Mr. Wright attends The University of North Texas as a painting and drawing major. He continues to make art a driving force of his life. *Finding Peace* represents Mr. Wright's second professional work as an artist.

(So that you don't have to damage your book,
permission to photocopy this form is granted.)

ORDER FORM

We hope you enjoyed this book from Polaire Publications.

If you would like to order additional copies of this book or other Polaire Publications books, please complete this form and send with payment to:

POLAIRE PUBLICATIONS
PMB 217, 2221 Justin Rd., Suite 119
Flower Mound, Texas 75028
or you may fax your order to (972) 691-9134
or visit www.animalcompanionsandtheirpeople.com

Name _____

Address _____

City, State, Zip _____

_____ No. books ordered   x $9.95   = $ _____
Shipping & Handling: $3.50 for
first book, plus $1.00 for
each additional book   = $ _____
           Subtotal   = $ _____
(Texas residents, please add 7.25% sales tax) = $ _____
           TOTAL   = $ _____

☐ Check: Please make payable to Polaire Publications.
☐ Credit Card: ☐ MasterCard   ☐ Visa

Card # _____ Exp. Date _____

Signature _____

$1 of each copy sold of books 1, 2, and 3 will be donated to:

SPCA OF TEXAS

Number of copies of each book ordered:

1. _____ When Your Pet Dies
2. _____ Animal Companions: Your Friends, Teachers & Guides
3. _____ Animal Companions In Our Hearts, Our Lives, and Our World
4. _____ Animal Elders: Caring About Our Aging Animal Companions
5. _____ Finding Peace After the Loss of a Loved Animal Companion